The Inside Story
Pyramid

Dana Meachen Rau

Marshall Cavendish
Benchmark
New York

Inside a Pyramid

1   entrance

2   room

3   stone blocks

4   tunnel

5   white stone

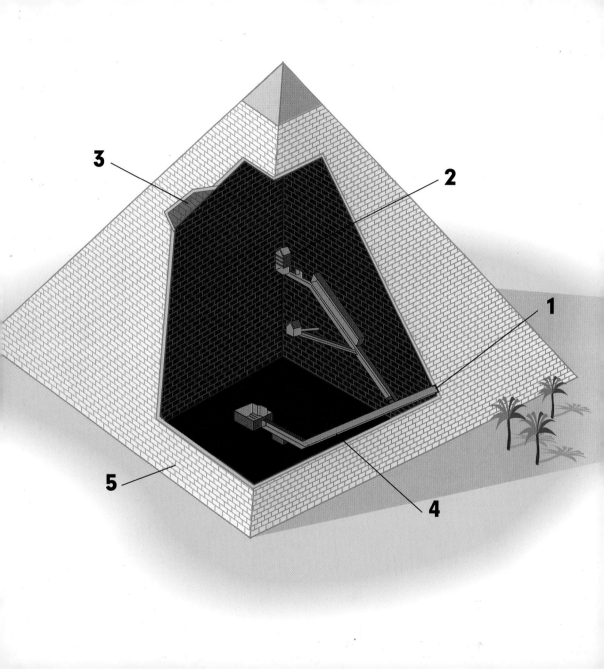

Pyramids are made of four triangles.

The triangles meet at the top.

In *Egypt*, workers built pyramids.

Pyramids are *tombs*.

A pyramid held a
pharaoh's body.

A *pharaoh* was a king.

A pyramid has *tunnels* inside.

The tunnels lead to rooms.

People painted pictures on the walls.

They filled the rooms with treasure.

Many workers built a pyramid.

First they made the ground flat.

Then they cut blocks of stone.

They cut the stone from the ground.

Workers pulled the heavy
blocks with ropes.

They rolled some blocks
on logs on the ground.

The workers set out the blocks.

They added more blocks on top.

The workers made ramps of hard mud.

They pulled the blocks up the ramps.

The pyramid grew taller.

They covered the sides
with white stone.

The pyramids have stood
a long time.

They are thousands of
years old.

Inside a Pyramid

blocks

pharaoh

ramp

tomb

tunnel **walls**

Challenge Words

Egypt (EE-jipt) A country in Africa.

pharaoh (FER-oh) A king in Egypt.

tombs (TOOMS) Places where bodies are put after people die.

tunnels (TUN-uhls) Hallways leading to rooms.

29

Index

Page numbers in **boldface** are illustrations.

About the Author

Dana Meachen Rau is an author, editor, and illustrator. A graduate of Trinity College in Hartford, Connecticut, she has written more than one hundred fifty books for children, including nonfiction, biographies, early readers, and historical fiction. She lives with her family in Burlington, Connecticut.

Reading Consultants

Nanci Vargus, Ed.D. is an Assistant Professor of Elementary Education at the University of Indianapolis.

Beth Walker Gambro received her M.S. Ed. Reading from the University of St. Francis, Joliet, Illinois.

With thanks to Nanci Vargus, Ed.D. and
Beth Walker Gambro, reading consultants

Marshall Cavendish Benchmark
Marshall Cavendish
99 White Plains Road
Tarrytown, New York 10591-9001
www.marshallcavendish.us

Text copyright © 2007 by Marshall Cavendish Corporation

Library of Congress Cataloging-in-Publication Data

Rau, Dana Meachen, 1971–
Pyramid / by Dana Meachen Rau.
p. cm. — (Bookworms. The inside story)
Summary: "Describes the architecture, construction,
and interior of a pyramid"—Provided by publisher.
Includes index.
ISBN-13: 978-0-7614-2275-4
ISBN-10: 0-7614-2275-7
1. Building, Stone—Egypt—History—To 332 B.C.—Juvenile literature.
2. Pyramids—Egypt—Design and construction—Juvenile literature.
3. Egypt—Antiquities—Juvenile literature.
4. Architecture, Ancient—Egypt—Juvenile literature. I. Title.
TH16.R38 2006
690'.68—dc22
2005031257

Photo Research by Anne Burns Images

Cover Photo by Getty Images

The photographs in this book are used with permission and through the courtesy of:
The Image Works: pp. 1, 25 CM Dixon/HIP; pp. 11, 29tl Werner Forman Archive;
p. 19 Mary Evans Picture Library. *Getty Images*: p. 5. *SuperStock*: pp. 7, 28br age fotostock.
Corbis: pp. 9, 28tr Sandro Vannini; pp. 13, 29tr Gianni Dagli Orti; pp. 15, 17, 28tl Roger Wood;
p. 27 Larry Lee Photography. *Bridgeman Art Library*: p. 21 Index, Barcelona, Spain;
pp. 23, 28bl Private Collection/Ancient Art & Architecture Collection.

Printed in Malaysia
1 3 5 6 4 2